BEANO®
PUZZLE BOOK

A STUDIO PRESS BOOK

First published in the UK in 2020 by Studio Press,
an imprint of Bonnier Books UK Limited,
4th Floor, Victoria House, Bloomsbury Square, London, WC1B 4DA
Owned by Bonnier Books,
Sveavägen 56, Stockholm, Sweden

www.bonnierbooks.co.uk
www.beano.com

A Beano Studios Product © DC Thomson Ltd (2020)

3 5 7 9 10 8 6 4 2

ISBN 978-1-78741-637-6

Edited by Sophie Blackman
Designed by Rob Ward
Artwork from Beano Puzzle Books,
1990–1994 from the Beano archive.

A CIP catalogue for this book is available from the British Library
Printed and bound in Great Britain by Clays Ltd, Elcograf S.p.A.

BEANO®
PUZZLE BOOK

ARE YOU ON A LONG JOURNEY,
STUCK IN A LIFT, OR JUST PLAIN BORED?

PICK UP YOUR PENCIL AND GET YOUR BRAIN JUICES
BUBBLING WITH THESE RETRO (THAT MEANS OLD
BUT STILL AWESOME) BEANO PUZZLES.

DENNIS AND HIS PALS HAVE TEAMED UP
WITH SOME OLD FACES AND HAVE MADE A
BOOK PACKED FULL OF THE MOST PUZZLING
PAGES IN BEANOTOWN HISTORY.

UNSCRAMBLE WORDS WITH WALTER, FIGURE
OUT NUMBERS WITH GNASHER, ESCAPE
MAZES WITH MINNIE AND MUCH MORE.

BEANOTOWN HAS NEVER BEEN SO PUZZLING!

SO BRING A DOLLOP OF DAFTNESS TO YOUR QUIET
DAYS AND HOLIDAYS AND GET SCRIBBLING!

IT WILL BE A-MAZE-ING.

HIDDEN IN EACH OF THE THREE SENTENCES BELOW IS THE NAME OF A CHARACTER. SEE IF YOU CAN FIND ALL THREE.

1. IF YOU CAN'T DRAW ALTER YOUR STYLE

2. GET EACH ERRAND BOY HERE

3. DON'T BE BRASH ERNEST

COME ON ALL MATHEMATICIANS – CAN YOU
HELP PLUG WITH THIS ONE? HE HAS TO PUT
ONE MULTIPLICATION SIGN AND SEVEN PLUS
SIGNS BETWEEN THE NUMBERS BELOW
TO GET AN ANSWER OF 100.

9 8 7 6 5 4 3 2 1 = 100

ANSWER
(9 × 8) + 7 + 6 + 5 + 4 + 3 + 2 + 1 = 100

IF YOU SOLVE THE CLUES OF THE CROSSWORD PROPERLY, THE SAME WORDS READ UP AND DOWN.

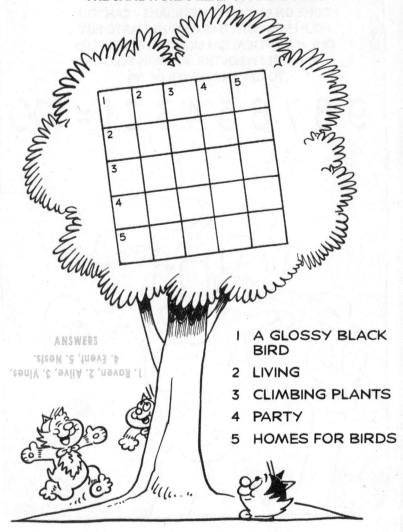

1 A GLOSSY BLACK BIRD
2 LIVING
3 CLIMBING PLANTS
4 PARTY
5 HOMES FOR BIRDS

FILL IN THE EMPTY BOXES WITH WORDS BEGINNING WITH 'CAR' THAT SUIT THE DEFINITIONS.

FAIR	
FLOWER	
VEHICLE	
JOINER	
VEGETABLE	
CHARCOAL	
SWEET	

SCOFF!

LOOK BEFORE YOU *LEAP* IS A WELL-KNOWN PROVERB. CAN YOU TURN *LOOK* INTO *LEAP* IN FIVE STEPS, CHANGING ONE LETTER TO FORM A NEW WORD AT EACH MOVE?

LOOK
___
___
___
___
LEAP

10

COPY THIS PICTURE OF THE THREE BEARS BY DRAWING YOUR LINES THROUGH THE SAME BOXES IN EXACTLY THE SAME PLACES.

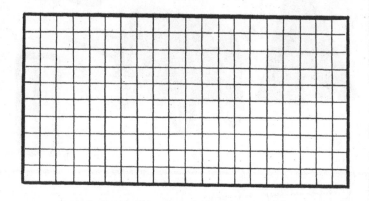

14

HELP JONAH TO UNSCRAMBLE EACH OF THE GROUPS OF LETTERS TO SPELL THE NAMES OF SIX SAILING CRAFT.

A YAKAK

B MAN CAT ARA

C GYHIND

D RINEL

E SIPH

F A MINER BUS

ANSWERS
A. Kayak, B. Catamaran, C. Dinghy, D. Liner,
E. Ship, F. Submarine.

WHICH TWO BITS OF WALL BELOW WILL FIT INTO LORD SNOOTY'S WALL TO FILL THE HOLE EXACTLY?

A.

B.

C.

D.

E.

18

SMIFFY HAS TO CROSS OUT NINE OF THESE FORTY LINES SO THAT THERE WILL BE NO SQUARES OF ANY SIZE LEFT. SEE IF YOU CAN HELP HIM.

ANSWER

One solution is to cross out lines 2, 10, 12, 13, 20, 21, 28, 31 and 34.

FIRST, USE ALL THE LETTERS IN 'BEST LAD' TO SPELL A SEVEN-LETTER WORD. THEN, DROP ONE LETTER AT A TIME AND REARRANGE THE REMAINING LETTERS TO SPELL A SIX, FIVE, FOUR, THREE, TWO AND, FINALLY, A ONE-LETTER WORD.

TEACHER WANTS THE BASH SREET KIDS TO WRITE THE GIVEN NUMBERS INTO THE EMPTY SQUARES ON THE RIGHT SO THAT THEY ADD TO TWENTY-EIGHT IN ALL ROWS ACROSS, DOWN AND DIAGONALLY.

1	2	3	4	5	6	7
1	2	3	4	5	6	7
1	2	3	4	5	6	7
1	2	3	4	5	6	7
1	2	3	4	5	6	7
1	2	3	4	5	6	7
1	2	3	4	5	6	7

A						
B						
C						
D						
E						
F						
G						

THUD!

FOXY IS HAVING A GREAT DREAM – ABOUT CHICKENS, WHAT ELSE? FOUR ARE DIFFERENT BUT TWO ARE THE SAME. CAN YOU SPOT WHICH TWO ARE THE SAME?

YIPES! TYPICAL CALAMITY JAMES! CAN YOU FIT ALL THE SOUND EFFECTS INTO THE CROSSWORD? 'SOUND EFFECTS' IS IN ITS CORRECT PLACE, TO GIVE YOU A START.

WHUMP
DONG
GURGLE

WALLOP
CLANK
SLURP

TINKLE
CLATTER
WHIZZ
THUMP

RATTLE
GRIND
HOWL
SPLAT

ZIP
PLOP
BOOM
THUNDER

CLANG
WHINE
PTCHING

CRACKLE
RUMBLE
SCREECH

23

KORKY'S KITS ARE CHASING SIX BIRDS HIDDEN IN THE BUSH. ADD ONE LINE TO EACH INCOMPLETE LETTER TO FIND OUT WHAT THE BIRDS ARE.

**DRAW IN YOUR OWN ENDING TO THE STORY
BELOW, THEN TURN OVER THE PAGE TO SEE IF
IT MATCHES BEANO'S VERSION.**

SEE IF YOU CAN CHANGE *HARD* TO *EASY* IN FIVE MOVES, CHANGING ONE LETTER TO FORM A NEW WORD AT EACH MOVE. PLUG FOUND IT HARD – BUT WALTER FOUND IT EASY!

HARD

EASY

ARE YOU ABLE TO WORK OUT THESE DAFT DOG BREEDS FROM THE DOTTY DRAWINGS?

CAIRN TERRIER, GREAT DANE, BULLDOG,

ABYSSINIAN WIRE-HAIRED TRIPE HOUND,

HUSKY, PEKINESE, POODLE,

AIREDALE, BOXER.

5.

6.

7.

8.

9.

ANSWERS

1. Airedale, 2. Puddle ... er, Poodle, 3. Great Dane, 4. Husky, 5. CAIRN terrier, 6. Peek-in-knees ... Pekinese, 7. Boxer, 8. Bulldog, 9. Gnasher – who is an Abyssinian wire-haired tripe hound.

29

HELP DINAH MO AND THE BURRD MATCH UP THE WORDS WITH THE PICTURES TO FIND THE NAMES OF SIX DIFFERENT KINDS OF BIRD.

30

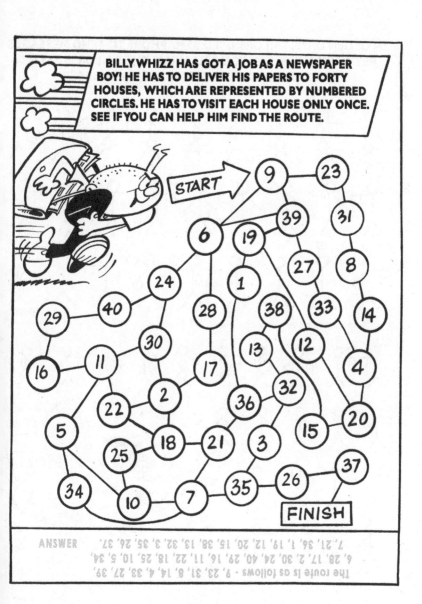

BILLY WHIZZ HAS GOT A JOB AS A NEWSPAPER BOY! HE HAS TO DELIVER HIS PAPERS TO FORTY HOUSES, WHICH ARE REPRESENTED BY NUMBERED CIRCLES. HE HAS TO VISIT EACH HOUSE ONLY ONCE. SEE IF YOU CAN HELP HIM FIND THE ROUTE.

ANSWER

The route is as follows - 9, 23, 31, 8, 14, 4, 33, 27, 39, 6, 28, 17, 2, 30, 24, 40, 29, 16, 11, 22, 18, 25, 10, 5, 34, 7, 21, 36, 1, 19, 12, 20, 15, 38, 13, 32, 3, 35, 26, 37.

IN OLDEN DAYS, SAILORS USED SEMAPHORE TO SEND MESSAGES BETWEEN SHIPS. CAN YOU TELL WHAT THE SAILOR IS SAYING IN THE MESSAGE BENEATH THE 'ALPHABET'?

ANSWER "Jonah has sunk our ship"

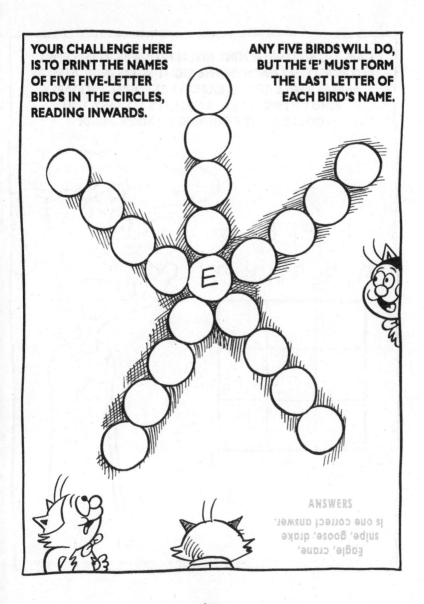

YOUR CHALLENGE HERE IS TO PRINT THE NAMES OF FIVE FIVE-LETTER BIRDS IN THE CIRCLES, READING INWARDS.

ANY FIVE BIRDS WILL DO, BUT THE 'E' MUST FORM THE LAST LETTER OF EACH BIRD'S NAME.

E

33

CAN YOU WRITE THE NINE GIVEN NUMBERS IN THE EMPTY
BOXES SO THAT EACH OF THE EIGHT ROWS INDICATED BY
ARROWS WILL ADD TO EXACTLY 2? YOU'LL PROBABLY
FIND IT 'TWO' EASY. IN FACT, IT'S SO EASY, YOU
COULD DO IT STANDING ON YOUR HEAD!

ANSWER

Row A: 1, $2/9$, $7/9$.

Row B: $4/9$, $6/9$, $8/9$.

Row C: $5/9$, $1 1/9$, $3/9$.

START AT A CERTAIN LETTER IN THE WORD SQUARE, AND MOVING TO THE NEXT LETTER IN A CERTAIN DIRECTION, SEE IF YOU CAN MAKE A THREE-WORD SENTENCE. THERE'S A CLUE IN THE PICTURE.

S	A	G	E	S
A	U	R	E	G
S	O	L	H	N
S	E	V	S	A

IVOR CHOPP
BUTCHER

BEST SAUSAGES TODAY

35

**IN BALLBOY'S DREAM HE CAN SEE SIX FOOTBALLS.
FOUR ARE THE SAME BUT TWO ARE DIFFERENT.
CAN YOU SPOT THEM?**

ANSWER   Numbers 2 and 5 are different.

HERE'S A GAME YOU AND YOUR PALS CAN PLAY. EACH PLAYER MUST TRY TO LEAD THE CRABS, ONE AT A TIME, TO THE NETS. WHOEVER CATCHES THE MOST CRABS IS THE WINNER. BE CAREFUL NOT TO LET ANY ESCAPE!

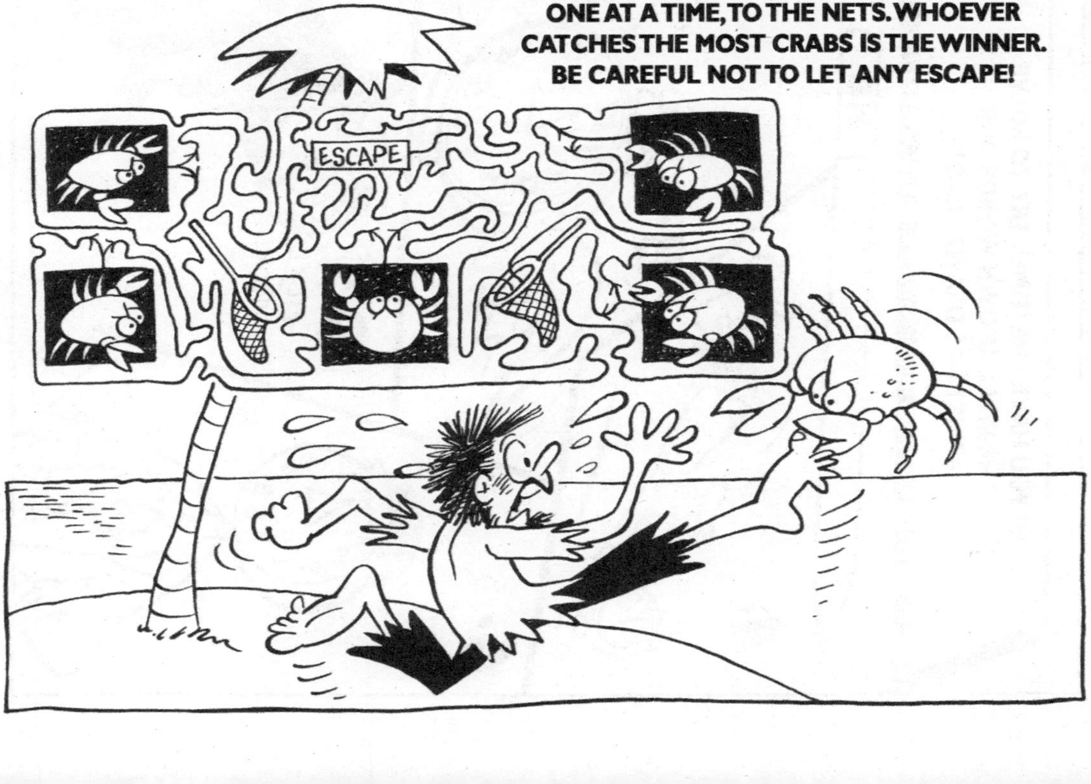

ESCAPE

IF YOU HAVE THE 'TIME', TRY TO SOLVE
THE WELL-KNOWN WORDS OUR
ARTIST HAS DRAWN BELOW!

RASHER WANTS YOU TO PRINT THE NAMES OF FIVE VEGETABLES IN THE ROWS HERE TO FIT IN WITH THE WORD 'ONION'.

CONNECT THE DOTS IN NUMERICAL ORDER
FROM 1 TO 48 AND YOU'LL SEE AN ANIMAL.

TRACE OVER THE NINE PIECES THAT MAKE UP THE DUCK BELOW. CUT THEM OUT, AND THEN SEE IF YOU CAN HELP DINAH MO FIT THEM TOGETHER AGAIN. IT'S NOT SO EASY – IT COULD DRIVE YOU QUACKERS!

TEACHER WANTS THE BASH STREET KIDS TO PUT THE GIVEN NUMBERS IN THE CIRCLES SO THAT THE THREE NUMBERS IN EACH STRAIGHT LINE WILL EQUAL SIXTY-SIX.

7 27 32 12 2 42 37 22 17

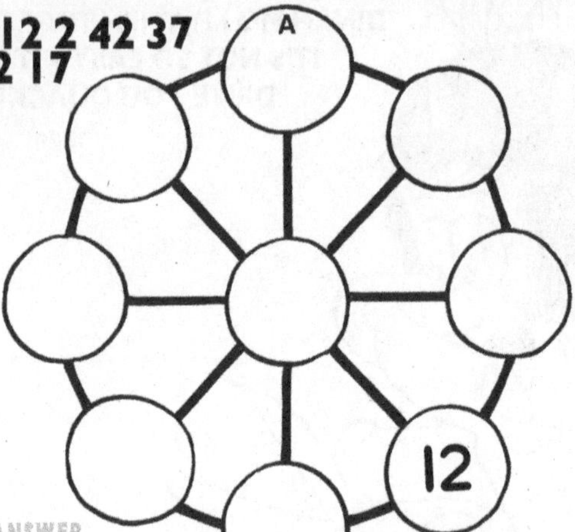

A

12

HIDDEN IN EACH OF THE THREE SENTENCES BELOW IS THE NAME OF A METAL. BRASSNECK SPOTTED THEM ALL – SEE IF YOU CAN DO THE SAME!

① THERE'S A BAT IN THE BELFRY

② GROWING OLD IS NOT SO BAD

③ A FOSSIL VERIFIES LIFE LONG AGO

HERE'S A GOOD DODGE TO BAFFLE YOUR FRIENDS WITH. FIRST OF ALL SHOW THEM A COIN IN THE BOTTOM OF A GLASS, AS IN FIG.1. THEN COVER THE GLASS WITH A HANDKERCHIEF, AS IN FIG.2.

WHEN YOU REMOVE THE HANDKERCHIEF THE COIN WILL HAVE VANISHED! HOW? BECAUSE IT WAS NEVER IN THE GLASS, BUT WAS HELD UNDERNEATH IT, AS IN FIG.3.

FIG 1.

FIG 2.

FIG 3.

← THE COIN

WHEN THE HANDKERCHIEF IS COVERING THE GLASS, IT IS EASY TO REMOVE THE COIN WITHOUT BEING NOTICED.

DRAW IN YOUR OWN ENDING TO THE STORY BELOW, THEN TURN OVER THE PAGE TO SEE IF IT MATCHES BEANO'S VERSION.

LES PRETEND HAS GOT A REAL BEE IN HIS BONNET
ABOUT THAT HONEY! HELP HIM THROUGH THE
MAZE BEFORE THE THREE BEARS GET THERE FIRST.

IN

HONEY OUT

P	A	M	S	A
G	T	N	L	F
I	S	A	C	V
W	R	P	H	N
L	T	C	S	O

START FROM CERTAIN LETTERS AND MOVE TO THE NEXT LETTER, IN ANY DIRECTION, TO SEE HOW MANY WORDS YOU CAN SPELL THAT RHYME WITH SNAP.

ANSWERS

zap, nap, chap, clap, lap, flap, slap, scrap, cap, rap, tap, trap, map, gap, wrap are 15.

HELP SMIFFY PRINT THE GIVEN NUMBERS IN THE FOURTEEN CIRCLES SO THAT EACH OF THE SEVEN ROWS EQUAL THIRTY-SEVEN.

7   8
9   10
11 12
13 14
15 16
17 18
19 20

USE THE FIFTEEN LETTERS GIVEN, EACH JUST ONCE, TO SPELL THE NAMES OF THREE GAMES PLAYED WITH A BALL.

UP TO FIVE PEOPLE CAN PLAY THIS GAME. ALL YOU HAVE TO DO IS CHOOSE A DOG AND THEN TRACE ALONG THE LINE LEADING FROM IT. WHOEVER REACHES THE BONE IS THE WINNER

EACH OF THE THREE SENTENCES BELOW CONTAINS A PRECIOUS STONE. SEE IF YOU CAN HELP THE BADD LADS FIND THEM.

54

WHICH FIVE SQUARES FROM THE SELECTION ON THE LEFT WILL FIT IN THE GAPS TO FINISH THE PICTURE OF A ROOTIN'-TOOTIN'-SHOOTIN' IVY THE TERRIBLE?

HOW BIG WAS THE FISH THAT KORKY NEARLY CAUGHT? JOIN THE DOTS IN NUMERICAL ORDER TO FIND OUT!

SMIFFY WANTS YOU TO PRINT THE NINE GIVEN NUMBERS IN THE CIRCLES SO THAT EACH OF THE FOUR ROWS EQUALS 120.

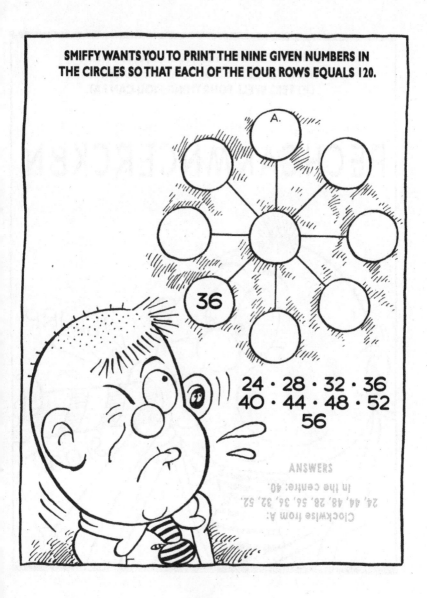

24 · 28 · 32 · 36
40 · 44 · 48 · 52
56

PRINT THE FIVE VOWELS, A, E, I, O, U, BETWEEN THE GIVEN LETTERS SO THAT THE COMBINED LETTERS SPELL FOUR THINGS YOU CAN EAT.

PECHCAKMNCERCKBN

SLURP!

SLOO!

SEE IF YOU CAN CHNAGE *MEAT* TO *BONE* IN FIVE MOVES, CHANGING ONE LETTER TO FORM A NEW WORD AT EACH MOVE.

59

TEACHER IS GIVING THE BASH STREET KIDS A GEOGRAPHY LESSON. HE WANTS THEM TO MATCH UP THE CITIES ON THE LEFT WITH THE COUNTRIES ON THE RIGHT. CAN YOU HELP?

A. MILAN	1. FRANCE
B. CADIZ	2. BELGIUM
C. NICE	3. ITALY
D. PORTO	4. MALTA
E. VALETTA	5. SPAIN
F. BRUGES	6. PORTUGAL

SQUELCH!

THUDD!

ANSWERS A/3, B/5, C/1, D/6, E/4, F/2.

IVY THE TERRIBLE HAS MOVED TO A NEW HOUSE AND SHE'S FOUND A WAY TO DRAW IT IN THREE EASY STAGES. SEE IF YOU CAN DO IT, TOO!

USE THE GIVEN LETTERS TO FORM FIVE DIFFERENT WORDS THAT WOULD COMPLETE THE TWO SENTENCES.

ANSWER

I lived near the Rio Grande with my ducks, geese and gander. They ranged my big garden where luckily there was no danger of drought.

A G N E D R

I LIVED NEAR THE
RIO _ _ _ _ _ _
WITH MY DUCKS, GEESE
AND _ _ _ _ _ _ _. THEY
_ _ _ _ _ _ _ MY BIG
_ _ _ _ _ _ WHERE LUCKILY
THERE WAS NO _ _ _ _ _ _
OF DROUGHT.

DRAW IN YOUR OWN ENDING TO THE STORY BELOW, THEN TURN OVER THE PAGE TO SEE IF IT MATCHES BEANO'S VERSION.

CAN YOU PUT THE NAME OF AN ARTICLE OF CLOTHING OVER EACH OF THE DASHES TO MAKE FIVE WELL-KNOWN TWO-WORD THINGS?

1 _ _ _ _ _ _ POTATO
2 _ _ _ _ _ _ COW
3 WIND _ _ _ _
4 _ _ _ _ HANGER
5 _ _ _ BREAK

BABY-FACE FINLAYSON FOUND THIS ONE CHILD'S PLAY! START FROM ANY LETER AND MOVE ALONG A LINE TO THE NEXT LETTER TO SEE HOW MANY THREE-LETTER WORDS YOU CAN SPELL.

MORE THAN 20 — GOOD
MORE THAN 25 — EXCELLENT.
MORE THAN 30 — MASTER MIND!

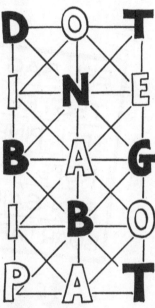

UNSCRAMBLE THE LETTERS TO FIND THE NAMES OF SIX BREEDS OF DOG THAT GNASHER HAS HAD A FIGHT WITH.

EEL BAG	
TESTER	
SEEK PINE	
ROPE TIN	
PEN SAIL	
BOAR LARD	

CHALLENGE YOUR PAL TO A GAME OF LEAP FROG! EACH CHOOSE A FROG TO LEAD TO THE POOL. TO DECIDE THE MOVES, TAKE TURNS TO FLIP A COIN. FOR HEADS, MOVE ONE DOT, AND FOR TAILS, MOVE THREE DOTS. THE FIRST FROG TO REACH THE POOL WINS!

GO BACK 3 DOTS

GO BACK 3 DOTS

JONAH WANTS YOU TO START AT CERTAIN LETTERS AND MOVE TO THE NEXT LETTER IN ANY DIRECTION TO SPELL AT LEAST THIRTEEN WORDS THAT RHYME WITH 'SAIL'.

70

CAN YOU HELP SMIFFY? HE HAS TO WRITE SINGLE NUMBERS INTO EACH EMPTY SQUARE SO THAT EACH ROW OF FIGURES ACROSS, DOWN AND DIAGONALLY WILL ADD TO NINETEEN.

CAN YOU NAME THE EIGHT FLOWERS THAT WALTER IS HOLDING, FROM THE LETTERS ON THE PETALS?

SEE IF YOU CAN CHANGE *WIND* TO *GUST* IN SIX MOVES, CHANGING ONE LETTER TO FORM A NEW WORD AT EACH MOVE.

ANSWER

Wind, wine, mine, mint,
mist, must, gust is one
way to do it.

WIND
_ _ _ _
_ _ _ _
_ _ _ _
_ _ _ _
_ _ _ _
GUST

**HERE IS A GRID DRAWING OF LORD SNOOTY.
SEE IF YOU CAN COPY IT EXACTLY
INTO THE EMPTY GRID BELOW.**

THE PUZZLE BOOK CHARACTERS ARE HAVING A PARTY,
AND ENJOYING IT BY THE LOOK OF THINGS! CAN YOU
SPELL AT LEAST TWELVE THREE-LETTER WORDS BY
USING ONLY THE LETTERS IN THE WORD 'PARTY'?

ANSWER

Par, pat, pay, pry, art, rap, ray, rat, tap, tar, try, yap are 13.

DINAH MO HAS A PARTY TRICK!
COPY THE WINDMILL SHAPE AT THE
BOTTOM OF THIS PAGE ONTO THICK
PAPER. MAKE THE SMALL CUTS
IN THE CENTRE, THEN PUSH IT
ONTO A DRINKING STRAW LIKE
YOU SEE BOTTOM RIGHT.

STIR A FULL GLASS OF LEMONADE THEN
POP IN THE 'WINDMILL' AND STRAW...
WATCH IT GO! TRY DIFFERENT GLASSES
WITH DIFFERENT LEVELS IN THEM AND
SEE WHICH ONE SPINS FOR THE LONGEST!

THIS ONE STUMPED SMIFFY... SEE IF YOU CAN GIVE HIM A HAND! HE HAS TO WRITE EIGHT 8S IN SUCH A WAY THAT THEY TOTAL EXACTLY 1000.

ANSWER
888 + 88 + 8 + 8 + 8 = 1000

SEE IF YOU CAN CHANGE *BROOM* TO *STICK* IN SEVEN MOVES, CHANGING ONE LETTER TO FORM A NEW WORD AT EACH MOVE. BY THE WAY, DO YOU RECOGNISE THE WITCHES?

BROOM
_ _ _ _ _
_ _ _ _ _
_ _ _ _ _
_ _ _ _ _
_ _ _ _ _
STICK

ANSWER

Broom, brook, crook, crock, clock, click, slick, stick is one way to do it.

GNASHER IS BEING PESTERED BY LOTS OF DIFFERENT KINDS
OF INSECTS, INCLUDING A MOSQUITO, CATERPILLAR, BEETLE,
EARWIG, MOTH, WASP, ANT, LOCUST, BUTTERFLY, HORNET
AND MOUSE. SEE IF YOU CAN FIT THEM AROUND
THE WORD 'GRASSHOPPER' IN THIS GRID.

WHICH TWO OF THE SIGNAL FLAGS THAT JONAH IS HOISTING ARE IDENTICAL? CAREFUL NOW – IT'S A LITTLE TRICKIER THAN IT LOOKS.

ANSWER
A and H, Jonah has hung "H" upside down!

CHANGE A LETTER IN EACH WORD TO SPELL THE NAMES OF SIX SEA FOODS THAT KORKY AND THE KITS WOULD LOVE TO EAT.

RASHER WANTS YOU TO COMPLETE SIX THREE-LETTER WORDS IN THE SQUARES READING DOWNWARDS BY PRINTING A SIX-LETTER VEGETABLE IN THE EMPTY SQUARES READING ACROSS.

A	C	S	B	A	J
E	T	Y	N	E	B

CAN YOU SPOT THE TWO IDENTICAL BOOKS ON CUTHBERT CRINGEWORTHY'S SHELF?

ANSWER
Numbers 8 and 29!

HELP LORD SNOOTY REARRANGE THE LETTERS TO FORM SIX TYPES OF HEADGEAR.

DRAW IN YOUR OWN ENDING TO THE STORY BELOW, THEN TURN OVER THE PAGE TO SEE IF IT MATCHES BEANO'S VERSION.

WALTER WAS NEEDING A GOOD WIND TO FLY HIS KITE – AND NOW HE'S GOT ONE!

SEE IF YOU CAN CHANGE *WIND* TO *KITE* IN FOUR MOVES, CHANGING ONE LETTER AT EACH MOVE TO FORM A NEW WORD.

WIND

_ _ _ _

_ _ _ _

_ _ _ _

KITE

ANSWER

Wind, mind, mine, mite, kite is one way to do it.

THIS IS A REAL ANGLER ENTANGLER. FIND OUT WHICH OF THE ANGLERS HAS CAUGHT THE FISH.

ANSWER
Minnie the Minx

TO WIN THIS MAZE GAME, YOU MUST LEAD AT LEAST TWO CHICKENS AWAY FROM FOXY TO SAFETY. START ONLY ONCE FROM EACH CHICKEN AND MOVE BETWEEN THE LINES.

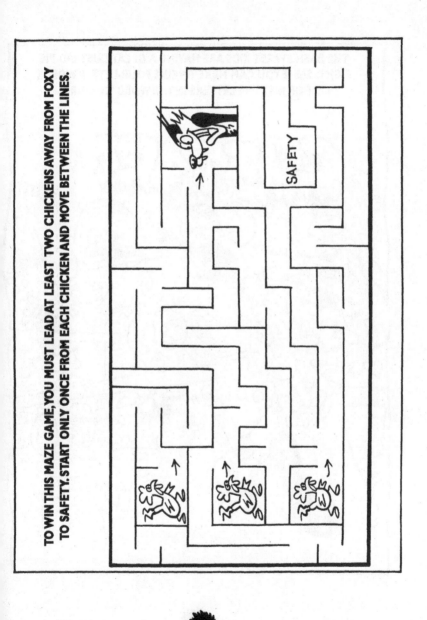

THE BASH STREET KIDS ARE HAVING A GREAT CUSTARD-PIE FIGHT. SEE IF YOU CAN MAKE TWELVE FOUR-LETTER WORDS OUT OF JUST THE LETTERS IN THE WORD 'CUSTARD'.

ANSWER

star, scar, cast, card, dust, rust, stud, curd, curt, cart, dart and duct are 12.

BELOW ARE FOUR EVERYDAY WORDS AS DRAWN BY OUR DAFT ARTIST. SEE IF YOU CAN WORK OUT WHAT THEY ARE MEANT TO BE.

ANSWERS

A: Selfish, B: Organise, C: Nestegg, D: Honeycomb.

SEE HOW QUICKLY YOU CAN FIGURE OUT WHICH THREE OF THESE NUMBERS WILL ADD TO EXACTLY 150.

BRASSNECK WANTS YOU TO PRINT THE NAMES OF FOUR DIFFERENT METALS, ONE LETTER OVER EACH DASH, SO THAT THE COMBINED LETTERS WILL SPELL OUT FOUR OTHER WORDS.

A
_ _ _ _ Y

B
_ _ _ _ _ ING

C
_ _ _ _ _ EN

D
_ _ _ _ _ _ SMITH

95

CHANGE ONE LETTER IN EACH OF THE WORDS BELOW TO SPELL OUT THE NAMES OF SEVEN TYPES OF TREE.

96

WALTER HAS DRAWN THIS CLOWN – BUT HE STILL HAS TO ADD A FACE. SEE IF YOU CAN HELP WALTER DRAW IN A FUNNY FACE.

GNASHER WANTS YOU TO SPELL OUT THE NAMES OF ELEVEN ANIMALS BY READING THE LETTERS AROUND THE CIRCLE IN THE DIRECTION OF THE ARROWS.

ANSWERS
Mule, doe, cat, fox, ox, camel, elk, pig, goat, cow and wolf.

TEACHER WANTS THE KIDS TO WRITE THE NINE NUMBERS HE HAS GIVEN THEM INTO THE EMPTY BOXES TO MAKE EACH OF THE EIGHT LINES TOTAL EIGHTEEN. SEE IF YOU CAN HELP.

2·3·4·5·6·7·8·9·10

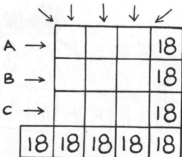

A →				18
B →				18
C →				18
18	18	18	18	18

99

PRINT A PUZZLE BOOK CHUM'S NAME IN THE EMPTY BOXES READING ACROSS TO COMPLETE THE THREE-LETTER WORDS READING DOWNWARDS.

PICK OUT THE FIVE BOXES ON THE LEFT-HAND SIDE THAT ARE NEEDED TO COMPLETE THIS FINE PICTURE OF BALLBOY.

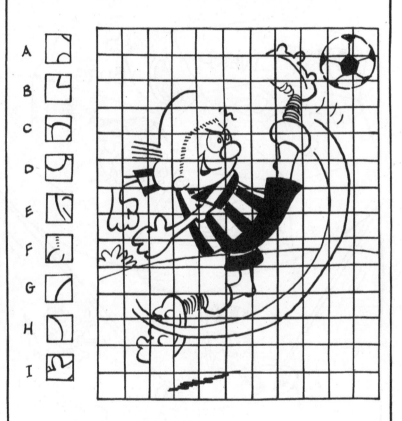

LORD SNOOTY IS GOING ON A TRIP ABROAD. FIND OUT THE NAMES OF THE TOWNS HE IS GOING TO VISIT.

DOG	FAWN
HARE	CUB
WOLF	PUP
DEER	FOAL
GOAT	LEVERET
HORSE	KID

LORD SNOOTY IS HAVING A FEW CHUMS AROUND TO CELEBRATE HIS BIRTHDAY. UNSCRAMBLE THE LETTERS TO FIND OUT WHAT IS FOR DINNER.

C ATUPSEN

D DEMON ALE

E SEW AND SICH

A CEI ACREM

B KETRYU

DENNIS SHOULD NEVER HAVE TAKEN A SHORTCUT ACROSS THE GOAT FIELD! IF YOU KEEP YOUR EYE ON THE PICTURE AND CONTINUE TO MOVE IT TOWARDS YOU AND AWAY FROM YOU, YOU WILL SEE THE GOAT HELP DENNIS ON HIS WAY!

MINNIE THE MINX WANTS TO TAKE UP A MUSICAL INSTRUMENT, SO SHE IS TRYING OUT A FEW TO FIND ONE SHE LIKES. UNSCRAMBLE THE LETTERS TO FIND OUT WHAT THEY ARE.

ANSWERS

1. Viola, 2. Flute, 3. Accordian, 4. Recorder, 5. Cello.

POOR OLD DENNIS IS REALLY IN THE SOUP – WALTER WANTS HIM TO RECITE THE ALPHABET BACKWARDS! CAN YOU DO IT? ONLY LOOK AT THE ANSWER IF YOU'RE REALLY STUCK!

ANSWER

Z,Y,X,W,V,U,T,S,R,Q,P,O,N,
M,L,K,J,I,H,G,F,E,D,C,B,A.

IVY THE TERRIBLE'S MUM TOOK HER TO THE ZOO. IF YOU JOIN THE DOTS IN NUMERICAL ORDER FROM 1 TO 50 YOU WILL SEE ONE OF THE ANIMALS SHE SAW.

DO NOT FEED THE ?

TWO DOGS ARE HIDDEN IN THIS PICTURE. CAN YOU HELP GNASHER AND GNIPPER FIND THEM?

ANSWER

IF FIVE CATS CATCH FIVE MICE IN FIVE MINUTES, HOW MANY CATS WILL YOU NEED TO CATCH ONE HUNDRED MICE IN ONE HUNDRED MINUTES?

ANSWER

It will require the same number of cats – that is, five cats!

110

CHIPS WANTS TO GET HOME BUT HE DOESN'T WANT TO BUMP INTO BULLY BEEF!
WITHOUT CROSSING A LINE, SEE IF YOU CAN FIND A SAFE ROUTE HOME FOR POOR CHIPS.

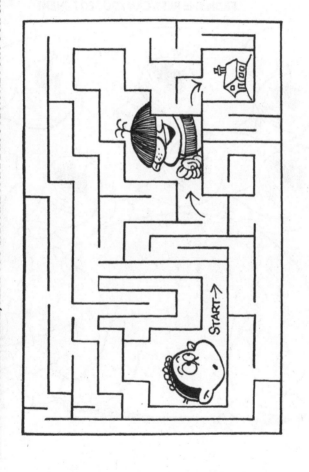

RASHER IS HAVING A GREAT DREAM – ABOUT TURNIPS, NATURALLY! HE CAN SEE SIX, BUT TWO ARE DIFFERENT FROM THE REST. CAN YOU SPOT THEM?

ANSWER
Turnips number 2 and 4 are different.

**JONAH IS CERTAINLY ON THE HIGH SEAS –
AND HE'S ON THE HIGH 'C's, TOO! HOW MANY
LETTER 'C's CAN YOU FIND IN THE PICTURE BELOW?**

ANSWER
There are 21 'C's.

GNASHER'S BITE IS WORSE THAN HIS BARK – AS WALTER FOUND OUT! CAN YOU CHANGE THE WORD *BARK* TO *BITE* IN FOUR MOVES, CHANGING ONE LETTER AT EACH MOVE TO FORM A NEW WORD?

BARK

_____

_____

_____

BITE

ANSWER
Bark, bare, bake, bike,
bite is one way to do it.

POOR DINAH MO IS STUCK IN THE MAZE! IF YOU START AT A CERTAIN LETTER AND MOVE TO THE NEXT LETTER IN ANY DIRECTION, YOU CAN SPELL A MESSSAGE THAT WIL LEAD HER OUT.

DENNIS IS PLAYING THE PANTOMIME FOOL AGAIN. HOW MANY WORDS WITH FOUR LETTERS OR MORE CAN YOU MAKE USING THE LETTERS OF THE WORD 'PANTOMIME'? AIM FOR AT LEAST FIFTEEN.

HERE IS A GRID DRAWING OF TOOTS. SEE IF YOU CAN COPY IT INTO THE EMPTY GRID EXACTLY.

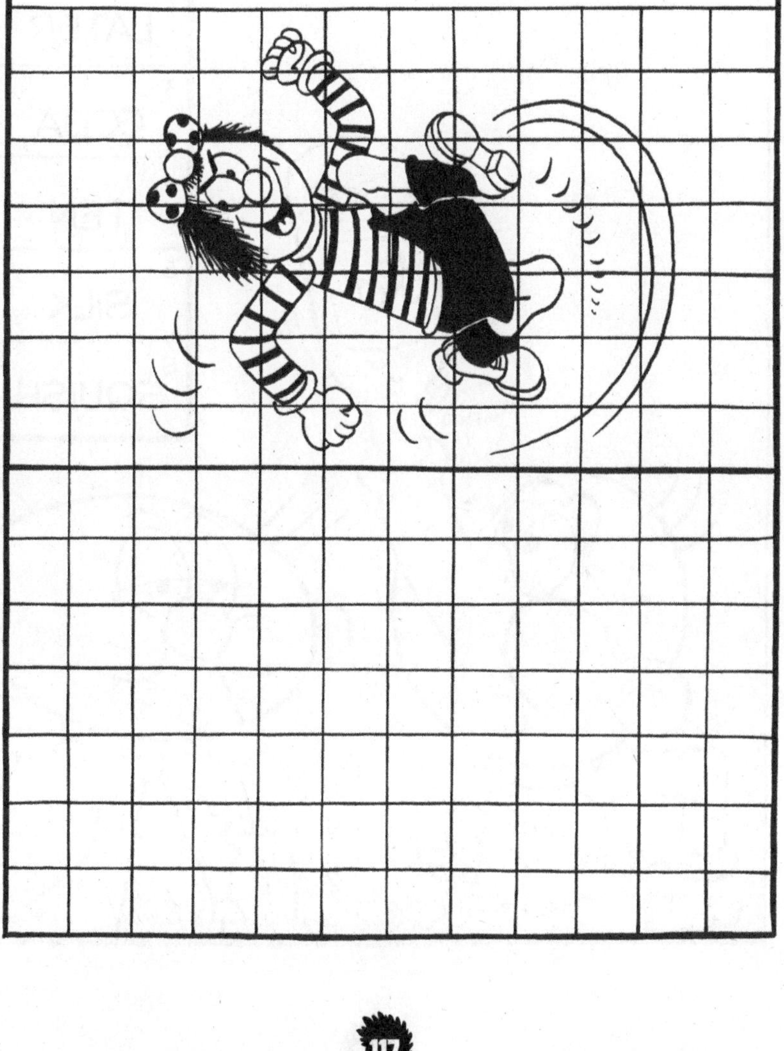

CHANGE ONE LETTER IN EACH WORD BELOW TO SPELL SIX THINGS WE CAN DRINK.

1	TOFFEE
2	LATER
3	CODA
4	TEN
5	SILK
6	SQUISH

ANSWERS

1. Coffee, 2. Water, 3. Soda, 4. Tea, 5. Milk, 6. Squash.

DRAW IN YOUR OWN ENDING TO THE STORY BELOW, THEN TURN OVER THE PAGE TO SEE IF IT MATCHES BEANO'S VERSION.

THIS ONE MADE SMIFFY CROSS-EYED. HE HAD TO WRITE THE NINE
GIVEN LETTERS IN THE CIRCLES TO FORM EIGHT THREE-LETTER
WORDS – FOUR WORDS THAT READ BOTH FORWARDS
AND BACKWARDS.

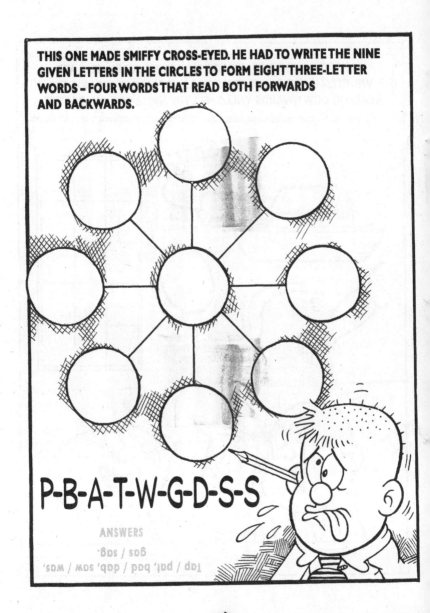

P-B-A-T-W-G-D-S-S

122

WHEN THE NAMES OF THE FIVE THINGS PICTURED HERE ARE WRITTEN IN THE RIGHT SEQUENCE, THE FIVE CENTRE LETTERS READING DOWNWARDS WILL SPELL THE NAME OF A CHARACTER.

IVY THE TERRIBLE IS A REAL BUNDLE OF MISCHIEF. SEE HOW MANY WORDS OF FOUR LETTERS OR MORE YOU CAN MAKE OUT OF THE LETTERS FOUND IN...

Terrible

CLONK!

DENNIS IS ON HOLIDAY AND HE'S LOOKING FOR A POSTCARD TO SEND TO GRAN! SEE IF YOU CAN CHANGE *POST* TO *CARD* IN FOUR MOVES, CHANGING ONE LETTER TO FORM A NEW WORD AT EACH MOVE.

POSTCARDS

POST

_ _ _ _

_ _ _ _

_ _ _ _

CARD

**SEE HOW WELL YOU CAN COPY THIS – AHEM! –
HANDSOME FACE IN THE EMPTY GRID ON THE RIGHT.**

TRACE OVER THE JUMBLED PIECES BELOW AND REARRANGE THEM WITHIN THE GRID SO THAT SPOTTY'S TIE BECOMES A SNAKE THAT WINDS THROUGH EVERY SQUARE.

ANSWER

THE NUMSKULLS HAVE GOT ALL MIXED-UP AND THEY'RE IN THE WRONG DEPARTMENTS! HELP SEND THEM TO THEIR USUAL PLACES BY SORTING OUT WHO SHOULD BE WHERE.

ANSWER

Brainy should be in the Brain department, Blinky in the Eye department, Radar in the Ear department, Snitch in the Nose department and Cruncher in the Mouth department.

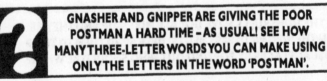

GNASHER AND GNIPPER ARE GIVING THE POOR POSTMAN A HARD TIME – AS USUAL! SEE HOW MANY THREE-LETTER WORDS YOU CAN MAKE USING ONLY THE LETTERS IN THE WORD 'POSTMAN'.

If you enjoyed *Your Life For Mine*, then why not try another gripping read from HQ Digital?

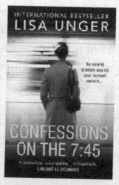

Dear Reader,

We hope you enjoyed reading this book. If you did, we'd be so appreciative if you left a review. It really helps us and the author to bring more books like this to you.

Here at HQ Digital we are dedicated to publishing fiction that will keep you turning the pages into the early hours. Don't want to miss a thing? To find out more about our books, promotions, discover exclusive content and enter competitions you can keep in touch in the following ways:

JOIN OUR COMMUNITY:

Sign up to our new email newsletter: hyperurl.co/hqnewsletter

Read our new blog www.hqstories.co.uk

https://twitter.com/HQDigitalUK

www.facebook.com/HQStories

BUDDING WRITER?

We're also looking for authors to join the HQ Digital family!
Find out more here:

https://www.hqstories.co.uk/want-to-write-for-us/

Thanks for reading, from the HQ Digital team